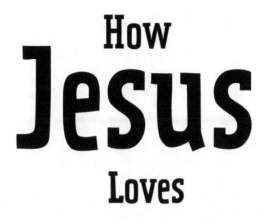

How
Jesus
Loves

31 devotions about Christ,
the cross and you

SINCLAIR B. FERGUSON

10 9 8 7 6 5 4 3 2 1

Copyright © 2022 Sinclair B. Ferguson
Hardback 978-1-5271-0858-5
EBook 978-1-5271-0927-8

Published by Christian Focus Publications,
Geanies House, Fearn, Tain, Ross-shire,
IV20 1TW, Scotland, U.K.
www.christianfocus.com;
email: info@christianfocus.com

Cover design and page layout by James Amour
Printed and bound by Gutenberg, Malta

CONTENTS

Introduction

If you go to church or Sunday school, maybe you have heard grown-ups speaking about how important it is to spend time each day with the Lord Jesus, and to think about him.

I don't know about you, but I find it hard just to sit down and think. Sometimes my head feels empty. But then, at other times, it feels as though there are too many things to think about! So, it's not easy just to sit down and say to yourself, 'I am going to think about Jesus for the next five minutes.'

What helps me is when I have something to think about—something that makes me think! So, reading a book helps me. Or if someone asks a question. It's a bit like starting the engine in the car—something needs to turn the key or press the starter button. You read and then you start thinking. Or you hear the question and you try to work out the answer—so you start thinking! I have tried to put these two things together in this book. I hope that reading it will start you thinking about Jesus. In addition, since each of its chapters begins with a question, I hope that will help you think even more about him. Don't forget to ask for his help by using the prayers.

When I was at school we hardly ever spoke in class. We spent a lot of time writing. So I find writing helps me to think. Not everybody likes writing. But if you do, why don't you keep a little book and write down your thoughts about Jesus while you are reading this book? Who knows, maybe one day you'll write a book like this one!

But until you write your own book, I hope you will enjoy the one I have written for you!

Sinclair B. Ferguson

1. JESUS KNOWS WHAT'S INSIDE

Lord Jesus,
help me to think about you, learn
more about you, and love you today.

READ: MATTHEW 23

Do you know what's inside of you? Have you ever seen underneath your skin or inside your bones?

When I was in Seoul, Korea one of my Korean friends said, 'Let's go to the Aquarium. I want you to see a very special fish.'

Now, I'm not really interested in fish, but my friend wanted me to see a very unusual fish. You could see all its bones! You could actually see right inside this fish.

As I walked away I thought: 'What would we humans be like if we were like that fish?'

If other people could look right inside us they would see all the bits that are working – the heart pumping and the blood going round. They might even be able to see inside our stomach and find out what we'd had for breakfast!

But think of this. Jesus is able to see right inside you, not to see what you have had for breakfast, but to see what you're thinking and see what you're wanting.

Have you ever seen an X-ray? It looks like a piece of thin plastic, but hold it up to the light and you can see inside your body. A doctor can take an X-ray of your heart, but Jesus sees right into the heart of our lives, where no one else can see –where he can see whether we love him or not.

I wonder if my heart is full of love for Jesus? Or is there something in my heart that's more important to me than Jesus? If there is, Jesus says, 'I'm going to have to fix that, if you're going to be really well as a Christian.'

We may say to Jesus, 'Don't do that, Jesus! I love that thing very much.' But he will say to us, 'If I don't fix it, it's going to do you a lot of damage. This is something that we need to fix.'

When Jesus fixes it we say, 'Ah, I'm much healthier now!'

The way to live happily with the Lord Jesus is to listen to what he says and to obey his Word.

Lord Jesus

Thank you for seeing the secrets of my heart and understanding everything about me. Please get rid of the things in my life that displease you and make me pure in your sight. I ask this in your name.

Amen.

Lord Jesus,
help me to think about you, learn
more about you, and love you today.

READ: GENESIS 19:1-26

Abraham had a nephew called Lot. He was well named! Lot wanted 'a lot'! When Abraham let him choose what land he would like, he chose the best looking land. But the people who lived there were horrible and did horrible things. They didn't love God, and they didn't want to do what God said. The place was called Sodom. It was horrible.

God sent a terrible judgement on Sodom. The earth shook and hot sulphur rained down from the sky. But God sent two angels to rescue Lot and his family.

God said, 'You must not stop. You must not look back.' But Mrs Lot did look back and she became a pillar of salt. All the sulphur rained down on top of her because she stopped.

I wonder why she looked back. Perhaps she wished that she hadn't left all her things behind. 'My jewels, my rings, that dolly I had when I was a little girl. Oh, they meant so much to me!'

Jesus said, 'Remember Lot's wife,' (Luke 17:32). When you decide to follow Jesus you can't look back. You've got to keep going. You can't give up.

A young woman called Gladys Aylward believed God was calling her to go to China. She asked some Christians, 'Will you send me to China?' She went from one group of Christians to another with the same question. Time after time she got the same answer. 'No, no! We can't send you to China.'

'But God has called me to go to China,' was Gladys' reply. 'If you're not going send me, I'll need to go to China on my own.' So that was what she did. She looked after little boys and girls who didn't have parents and she taught them about the Lord Jesus.

Gladys was faithful to the Lord Jesus. Some people had said to her, 'It's too difficult to go.' But Gladys said, 'If God has told me to go, then I'm going.'

That's the way to live. When God tells you to go and you go, he blesses you. He keeps you and he guides you and he uses you. Gladys Aylward helped many people. Do you think you would be willing to go? It might just be to somebody in school or, it might be to faraway China. When God says, 'Go!' go.

Loving Heavenly Father

We thank you for your Word that tells us to go into all the world and make disciples of all nations. Please help us at home and with our friends to tell them about you. Help us to go because you have told us. We ask this in Jesus' name.

Amen.

3. FOLLOW THE WAY

Lord Jesus,
help me to think about you, learn
more about you, and love you today.

READ: ACTS 24:10–16; JOHN 14:6

One day I was reading the local newspaper when I saw an advert that caught my eye. It said, 'Ask Saint Jude for three favours.' What does that mean? I think it means that you're supposed to ask Saint Jude for something special to happen.

Perhaps you've heard of people who say special prayers to Mary for nine days. A 'novena' is a prayer that some people say for nine days in succession.

Don't you think it is a big mistake to pray to Mary or Jude when our Father God wants us to pray to him?

Jesus says, 'Pray in my name. I am the Way to the Father' (See John 14:6).

Perhaps these people think that Jesus is too busy? Maybe they think to themselves, 'I'm afraid of Jesus, I'd better go to somebody else.'

The world is full of people who don't know the Way. Paul said he was a follower of the Way, the one and only Way to get to God. And who is the Way? The Way to God is the Lord Jesus Christ.

When Paul spoke about being a follower of the Way, he was speaking about being a follower of Jesus, because Jesus is the Way to get to know God.

If we know the Way we should tell others about him! Tell somebody who doesn't know Jesus that he is the Way to God.

If we're following Jesus, loving Jesus, serving Jesus, trusting Jesus, we will want to get to know Jesus better!

But lots of your friends don't know the Way. They're lost! Let's pray to the Lord Jesus and say, 'Help me to tell my friends about you.'

Jesus will answer that prayer.

Lord Jesus

We thank you that you are the Way, and the Truth and the Life. You are the Way to know our Heavenly Father. You give us new life and power to serve you. Please help us to tell our friends about you. Help us always to follow you, serve you, please you and love you. We pray this for your name's sake.

Amen.

4. HOW MANY BIRTHDAYS?

Lord Jesus,
help me to think about you, learn
more about you, and love you today.

READ: JOHN 3: 1-16

How many birthdays do you have? You only have one birthday. However, somebody in the United Kingdom has two. The British Monarch has an official birthday and an actual birthday. But you and I have only got one birthday.

Do you remember anything about the day you were born? Can you remember what happened? Of course you don't. You might have been told about it, or seen photographs, but you won't remember the day at all.

One night a man called Nicodemus came to see Jesus. He wanted to find out about belonging to the kingdom of God. He wanted to speak to Jesus about being part of God's family.

Jesus said to him, 'Nicodemus, you'll never be part of God's family until you've had two birthdays.'

Now Nicodemus couldn't work this out. He said to Jesus, 'But I'm quite an old man. I can't shrink right back to the beginning again so that I can have another birthday! How can I possibly have two birthdays? Why do I need to have two birthdays if I'm going to be in God's family?'

Jesus said to him, 'Nicodemus, you need to have two birthdays. You had one birthday when you were born into your own family. But if you're going to be born into God's family, you'll need to have another birthday.'

Nicodemus said, 'I don't think I understand that, Jesus.' So Jesus explained it to him. 'This second birthday can be yours when the Holy Spirit works in your heart and you are born again.'

When babies are born, how do you know that the baby is alive? Babies cry – and that's how you know that they're alive. Babies usually cry when they want to be fed which is another sign that the baby is alive. The baby is beginning to grow and needs to have food. That's why babies cry – loudly!

Being born again is a bit like that. The first sign that you've been born again is that you cry out to God and you call him 'Father'. When we call God 'Father, Dear Father' – that's one of the signs that the Holy Spirit has worked in our hearts so that we belong to God's family.

Jesus said, 'When you call my Father, 'Heavenly Father' and you love him and trust him, that's the sign that the Spirit has given you another birthday.'

So, although you have one birthday, it is possible to have two. If you love and trust in Jesus then you will have had a second birthday. Maybe you won't remember anything about it, but if you trust in the Lord Jesus Christ, the Holy Spirit has begun to work in your heart. When you are asked when your birthday is, you can say, 'Well, I've got the birthday when I came into the world. And because I love the Lord Jesus and trust the Heavenly Father, I have had another birthday.'

Lord Jesus

We thank you that you give us new life as well as ordinary life. Please help us to know your Father and our Father better and to trust you more. Bless our families and help us all to love and serve and worship you together. We pray this in your name.

Amen.

5. AN ETHIOPIAN VISITOR

Lord Jesus,
help me to think about you, learn
more about you, and love you today.

READ: ACTS 8:26-40

When Jesus went back into heaven, he sent the Holy Spirit to the church. Christians then started going to all kinds of different places, telling people about Jesus. A man called Philip went to Samaria where many people became Christians. But then God did a strange thing. Instead of keeping Philip in a place where so many people were becoming Christians – he sent him to a place where there was nobody! Well, almost nobody.

Philip was sent to the Gaza desert. There he saw a chariot belonging to a man from the country of Ethiopia. The man was reading something out loud.

He was reading from Isaiah, Chapter 53, about a man who was taken like a lamb to be killed and didn't say anything:

> He was oppressed, and he was afflicted, yet
> he opened not his mouth; like a lamb that
> is led to the slaughter, and like a sheep that
> before its shearers is silent, so he opened
> not his mouth (Isaiah 53:7 ESV).

The Holy Spirit told Philip to catch up with the chariot. So he ran up alongside it and called over to the Ethiopian, 'Do you understand what that is all about?'

The Ethiopian looked at him and said, 'No I don't. I need someone to explain it to me.' So, he invited Philip to come up and sit beside him in the chariot.

This Ethiopian man had been to Jerusalem to worship God. He even had his own copy of the Book of Isaiah. However, he still didn't know the Lord Jesus. So Philip sat down beside him and said, 'I need to tell you something. It's not just reading your Bible that's important. It's knowing and trusting Jesus. Isaiah is talking here about Jesus.' Philip told him all about Jesus, and the man from Ethiopia became a Christian.

When I was your age, I read my Bible day after day and I thought that that's what it meant to be a Christian. I thought that to be a Christian you had to read your Bible, say a prayer and sometimes help an old lady across the road. Although I was reading my Bible, I still didn't know Jesus or trust in him.

Then I read John, Chapter 5, verses 39–40 (ESV). As I read them, it was as if a light had been turned on! Jesus said this: 'You search the Scriptures because you think that in them you have eternal life; and it is they that bear witness about me, yet you refuse to come to me that you may have life.'

That was what I was missing. I hadn't really been trusting in Jesus at all.

Now here's a question for you. We read the Bible in church. We read the Bible in Sunday School. Maybe we also read the Bible at home. But are we trusting the Lord Jesus? Are we living for him?

Lord Jesus

Thank you for giving us the Bible. Thank you that we may come to you. As we read your Word, may we learn to trust in you, to love you and to want to serve you. We pray this in your name.

Amen.

6. GET IN A TIME MACHINE

Lord Jesus,
help me to think about you, learn
more about you, and love you today.

READ: GALATIANS 6:12–18

I want you to imagine that you can get into a great big time machine. You are going to go back in time to the year A.D. 100 and still keep travelling until you stop somewhere about the year A.D. 50. Imagine you're at the church that Paul was a member of in Antioch. They are just about to have a church picnic.

Antioch is near the Mediterranean Sea where it's nice and warm. Because all the children are playing they are feeling quite hot and sweaty. Some of the adults are also feeling the heat. Most of the men have rolled up their sleeves.

Do you notice that the Apostle Paul has done the same? What's that you see on his arms?

They look like bruises. And look at his legs – they have scars all over them. You turn and say to someone, 'What happened to him?'

An older boy whispers to you, 'The Apostle Paul was telling people about Jesus and some of them attacked him. They threw great big stones at him. He was almost killed.'

Later on in the afternoon you sit down near Paul. He is re-reading a letter. Just at the end, he had written these words:

> 'I bear in my body the marks of the Lord Jesus' (Galatians 6:17).

You realise that Paul is willing to die for the Lord Jesus. You want to ask him all kinds of questions. Oh dear, it's time for you to leave Bible times and come back to the twenty-first century!

Before Paul became a Christian he was known as Saul of Tarsus. But can you remember the name of the man who was ready to die for the Lord Jesus in order that Saul of Tarsus might become a Christian? His name was Stephen. When he was being stoned to death Saul actually looked after the coats of the people who were throwing the stones.

As he looked on perhaps Saul thought, 'That man must really love Jesus if he's willing to die for him. I wonder if what he said about Jesus is really true?'

Later, on the road to Damascus, Saul discovered for himself that it was true. Stephen had been prepared to die so that Saul would become a Christian. Years later when Saul was known by his Roman name, Paul, he too was prepared to die so that others would come to know Jesus Christ as their Lord and Saviour.

I don't suppose that people will often throw things at you because you're a Christian. But sometimes people may be nasty. Remember this: sometimes the people who are mad at you for loving Jesus are the very people that God is going to change. So be faithful and be brave. Your enemies may one day become friends of Jesus.

Lord Jesus

Thank you for dying for us and for giving courage to Stephen and Paul. Please give us courage and strength. Make us brave enough to be your witnesses. We pray this in your name.

Amen.

7. PAUL IN TROUBLE

*Lord Jesus,
help me to think about you, learn
more about you, and love you today.*

READ: ACTS 16:16–34

Paul always seemed to get into trouble. Often when he preached about Jesus somebody got angry with him or beat him up or tried to stone him to death.

When Paul came to Philippi he told the people there about the Lord Jesus. Some were delighted. They had never heard about Jesus before. They came to trust in Jesus as their Saviour. But wherever Paul went there were always some people who wanted to stop him speaking about Jesus.

This is what happened in Philippi. However, this time his friend, Silas, was with him. The two men were thrown into the jail and had their legs fastened in the stocks so that they wouldn't escape. That must have been horrible for them! But even all these horrible things didn't stop them from singing hymns to God. They were still singing hymns at midnight when an earthquake struck.

The jailer was terrified. He rushed up to Paul and asked 'What must I do to be saved by Jesus?'

Paul and Silas told him to trust in Jesus. That night the jailer became a Christian.

Sometimes people are brought to trust in the Lord Jesus by what we say about him. However, they can also be brought to Jesus by watching us and seeing what we do when things go wrong.

Everything seemed to be going wrong for Paul and Silas. But when they were stuck in the stocks what did they do? They turned to each other and they said, 'Let's praise Jesus because he's such a wonderful Saviour.'

When the earthquake began, Paul and Silas were sore, beaten, lonely men in a horrid prison, but they still sang praises about Jesus. When the jailer saw that perhaps he thought, 'What an amazing Saviour this Jesus must be!'

How is it possible to sing God's praises when things are going wrong? The only way you can do it is if the Lord Jesus is living in your life. When things begin to go wrong, you can still praise him. Then your friends will say, 'Why is it that she praises Jesus all the time?'

Maybe they'll be like that Philippian jailer and they'll ask you how to be saved by Jesus.

Let's pray that, like Paul and Silas, we'll be able to praise the Lord Jesus so that others will get to know him through us.

Lord Jesus

We thank you that you were with Paul and Silas in prison. We thank you for what you did in the heart of the jailer. Sometimes people are not nice to us, but help us to keep on praising you so that they will see that you really are a wonderful Lord and a great Saviour. We ask this in your name.

Amen.

Lord Jesus,
help me to think about you, learn
more about you, and love you today.

READ: Acts 7:54-59

Do you know what age you need to be to vote? You have to be eighteen to vote in the United Kingdom or in the United States of America.

In Acts Chapter 7, we are told that Paul cast his vote against the Christians. He said, 'I don't want the Christians.' This was before he believed in Jesus Christ of course. People knew him then as Saul of Tarsus. When he was asked, 'Will we let this Christian called Stephen live?' Saul said, 'Let's stone him!' They did. The men had to take their coats off to do it and they said to Saul, 'You watch my coat.' Paul didn't mind doing that. He hated Christians.

But someone else had a vote. When Saul went off to find more Christians to stone to death, Jesus had already decided on his vote. Saul was murdering all these Christians who trusted in Jesus and followed him. How do you think Jesus had voted? Did he say, 'Saul must die' or did he say, 'Let him live'? When Jesus voted, he voted 'Live!'

Saul was on the way to Damascus when Jesus met him. A bright light blinded him. Saul said, 'Lord, who are you?'

Jesus showed Saul mercy and Saul came to know Jesus Christ as his Lord and Saviour. Even though Saul had voted against Jesus and his followers, Jesus had already voted for Saul. He had died for Saul. He forgave him and brought him into the family of God.

We have got to vote about something too. We've got to vote about Jesus. What will your vote be? Will it be 'No, I don't want you, Jesus'? Or will it be 'Yes! I want to trust Jesus and to love Jesus and to live for Jesus'?

Thankfully you don't need to be eighteen to vote about this. You can trust in Jesus at any age. You can tell Jesus you love him at any time.

'Yes, Jesus. I trust you and love you and want to serve you.'

Lord Jesus

We want to say, 'Yes!' to you. We want to live for you. Please give us the strength, courage and help that we need. Please give us the joy that you've promised us, to live every day of our lives, saying 'yes' to you and 'yes' to everything you tell us. We ask this in your great name.

Amen.

9. A MAN BORN BLIND

*Lord Jesus,
help me to think about you, learn
more about you, and love you today.*

READ: JOHN 9:1-12; GENESIS 2:7

How do blind people read when they can't see the letters? They use Braille. They use their fingers to feel little raised up dots on the page. Somehow or other people who have no sight develop tremendous powers of touching as well as hearing.

When people lose their sight sometimes they learn to use their other senses better than they did before. These senses often become stronger to make up for the ones they don't have.

One day Jesus met a man who had been blind from birth. He couldn't see a thing. He heard Jesus getting down on his knees. Jesus picked up some dirt and spat on it. He made the dirt into a kind of paste and then told the blind man to 'Hold still.'

He dabbed the paste all over the man's eyes. Then he said, 'Go to the pool of Siloam. Wash your eyes and then you'll be able to see.'

The man did as he was told and went to the pool of Siloam. He washed his eyes and then for the first time in his life he was able to see.

Now Jesus could have made that blind man see by just saying, 'You can see now, go home.' So why did he go to all the bother of making a paste and dabbing it on the man's eyes?

Right at the beginning the Bible tells us how God made human beings out of mud.

> And the LORD God formed man of the dust of the ground, and breathed into his nostrils the breath of life, and man became a living being (Genesis 2:7).

I think Jesus used the mud to teach the blind man (and us) that we need to be remade. We need to be made new. That was why Jesus came into the world. He came to make people new. Isn't that wonderful? Jesus has come into the world to pick up the pieces of our lives that have been broken by our sin and other people's sin. If you are ever walking in the mud remember what Jesus could do with mud.

Lord Jesus

Thank you for the amazing things that you are able to do. Please make our lives new all over again. Help us to live, like that blind man, for your praise and glory. We thank you that you are the Light of the world. We want to follow you all of our lives. This we pray in your name.

Amen.

10. WHO DO YOU WANT?

Lord Jesus,
help me to think about you, learn
more about you, and love you today.

READ: ACTS 1:3-8

Imagine it's lunchtime and there is an extra seat at the table with a knife and a fork and maybe a spoon. You say to Mum or to Dad, 'Who's coming to lunch today?'

Then Mum says to you, 'Anybody you want. You can have anybody you want to come to lunch today. Anybody famous, anybody from history that you've read about.' What would you say to her? Who would you like to have?

For about six weeks after Jesus' crucifixion, the disciples had the wonderful experience of Jesus visiting them regularly. If you had asked them who was coming to lunch – they'd have said 'Jesus.' How could this be if he had just died? Jesus had risen from the dead, and for weeks he kept turning up again.

Why do you think he did this? He wanted to teach them more about what he had done.

Now if you had Jesus with you to lunch, you'd have lots of questions to ask him. How did you walk on the water? How did you still the storm? The disciples would have had a lot of questions too. But Jesus was really preparing them for the time when he would leave to go back to his Father in heaven.

There was one important lesson that Jesus wanted to teach them. Jesus had said a very strange thing before he died: 'It's going to be better for you that I leave you.' How could it possibly be better for them if Jesus went? That's hard to understand, isn't it?

This is what Jesus taught them: 'I'm going to go away and then in my place I'm going to send you the Holy Spirit.'

Do you remember when Jesus was born, it was because of the work of the Holy Spirit? When Jesus was tempted he overcame the temptations through the power of the Holy Spirit. All the miracles and mighty deeds that Jesus did - he did in the power of the Holy Spirit. When he died on the cross, the Holy Spirit was with him, giving him strength so that he could go through the pain. And when he rose from the dead, the Bible tells us that the power of the Holy Spirit was at work.

So right from the moment that Jesus was just a tiny baby, all the way through his life the Holy Spirit had been with him.

When it was finally time for him to leave his disciples, he said, 'I am going to give you the Holy Spirit who was with me for all of those years. He's going to come and live in your lives and because he has been with me all these years, it will be just like having me in your heart.'

So, when the Holy Spirit is in your life, it is like having Jesus with you, everywhere you go! This is absolutely amazing. The same Holy Spirit who helped Jesus has come to help us too.

Lord Jesus

It's hard for us to think that there could be anything better in all the world than having you with us at lunchtime. We thank you that you have given us someone else. You've given us your own Holy Spirit to be with us forever and to bring us close to you. We thank you and we praise you.

Amen.

11. EXPENSIVE BIBLES!

*Lord Jesus,
help me to think about you, learn
more about you, and love you today.*

READ: PSALM 119:99, ISAIAH 50:4.

Do you own a lot of books or magazines? Perhaps you own a tablet, or listen to audio books? Jesus probably did not own a single book. He didn't even have a Bible. To own a Bible in Jesus' day you would have had to have lots of money. Bibles were so expensive! There was no printing and no computers. People wrote things out slowly and paper cost a lot.

One day some people who were jealous of Jesus said to him, 'How do you know so much when you don't have any books?' The answer was that Jesus had listened to the reading of the Bible, and had memorised as much of it as he possibly could.

Psalm 119 was helpful to him. It is the longest Psalm in the Bible. It was written in a way that helped Hebrew boys and girls to memorise it. The psalm was divided into sections. Each section began with a different letter of the Hebrew alphabet – starting at the first letter and then going through to the last letter. Each verse in the section then began with that same letter.

Psalm 119:99 says: 'I have more understanding than all my teachers, for Your testimonies are my meditation.'

There were people in Jesus' day who had read all about God. But because Jesus trusted his Heavenly Father and thought about what God said he knew far more than them. In fact, when Jesus was twelve years old, the teachers were amazed that he could answer questions about the Bible that they had been puzzled about for years.

Isaiah 50:4 says something that was true of Jesus: 'He awakens Me morning by morning, He awakens My ear to hear as the learned.'

Jesus knew so much because he loved his Father and loved listening to him. Every morning he would be thinking, 'How can I do the things that my Father wants me to do?'

Here is a promise: Listen to what God says in his Word. Every morning wake up and wonder, 'How can I do what my Heavenly Father wants me to do today?' In a few years – it's a guarantee – you will know more than some of your teachers!

Loving Heavenly Father

Thank you for your Word, the Bible. Help me to read it each day and memorise it. Help me to learn more about you and how you want me to live. Teach me how to become more like you and help me to understand what you are saying to me. I ask this for your sake.

Amen.

12. A BIBLE ARCHITECT

Lord Jesus,
help me to think about you, learn
more about you, and love you today.

READ: 1 CORINTHIANS 3:16

Do you know what architects do? They design buildings. There is a wonderful church building in the centre of the city of Glasgow. It was designed by an architect whose name was William Stark. When it was first built you came out of the back door and there were green fields. But now it's in the middle of a large city. All you can see are large buildings, shops, restaurants, traffic and lots of people.

Now, the church building is not enormous. There are other buildings that are far bigger. Is it very tall? No – skyscrapers in New York are much, much taller. However, the architect who designed the church made it a special size. Can you guess what size he made it? Let me give you a clue.

In the Bible we read about another architect, King Solomon. He built the temple in Jerusalem. This was a special building for God. God's people went there to worship him. God would come to the temple to meet with them.

When Solomon built the temple, people didn't measure things in metres or yards. They used a measurement called a cubit. When Solomon built his temple, it was sixty cubits long by twenty cubits wide. A cubit was about eighteen inches or forty-five centimetres.

Now, here is something I found very interesting. The church is about the same size as Solomon's temple. Isn't that amazing! Did Mr Stark want to remind this congregation that they belonged to the same church as the Old Testament believers?

The apostle Paul tells us in 1 Corinthians 3: 16 that there is something even more amazing than these buildings. Paul said, 'God is now building a much better temple that is going to spread all over the world. You are God's temple.' Peter says, 'God isn't using ordinary stones any longer – he's using living stones – men and women, boys and girls and he's fitting them all together.'

When we all fit together in the church family, we become God's temple. God comes and meets with us and we praise him and we worship him and we love him.

God meets with his people – even if we don't have a building! God will meet with his people wherever they meet together.

Lord Jesus

Thank you for all the people who have trusted you as their Saviour. We praise you that you meet with us when we come to church. Help us to love you. Thank you that we belong to you and to each other. We pray in your name.

Amen.

13. THE BIGGEST PROMISE

Lord Jesus,
help me to think about you, learn
more about you, and love you today.

READ: 2 CORINTHIANS 1:20

Do you know what a 'high five' is? You see it when you watch a basketball game on television or an American sport like baseball.

When somebody hits a home run in baseball and the ball goes off the field, the player will go back to the dugout and he'll raise his hand up. His team mates will then smack their hands against his! And sometimes they'll shout, 'Yes!'

When they do this they mean, 'We've done it!'

God has made lots of promises. The Bible is full of them. But how do we know that God is going to keep his promises? Here is the answer:

> For all the promises of God find their Yes
> in him [Jesus]. That is why it is through
> him that we utter our Amen to God for his
> glory (2 Corinthians 1:20 ESV).

We know that God will keep all his promises because he kept the biggest promise of all. The biggest promise that our Heavenly Father has made is that he would send his own Son, Jesus, to die on the cross so that our sins would be forgiven.

When Jesus was dying on the cross, right at the end, he asked for a little drink. He was so tired and it was so difficult for him to speak. He was so thirsty!

> After this, Jesus, knowing that all was now
> finished, said (to fulfill the Scripture),
> 'I thirst' (John 19:28 ESV).

Somebody came and gave him something to drink, so that his mouth wouldn't be dry and so that he could speak. Then, in a very loud voice he said, 'It is finished!' What he meant was 'Yes! I've done it'. He had died for all of our sins on the cross. God's biggest promise, that he would send Jesus to be our Saviour, had been kept.

Because God has kept his biggest promise, we can be absolutely sure that he will say, 'Yes!' to all his other promises too.

Lord Jesus

Thank you for showing us that God the Father keeps his promises. Help us to remember that you kept your greatest promise and that all your promises will have the answer 'yes'. We pray that you'll be with us today. And we pray in your name.

Amen.

14. USING A LETTER INSTEAD OF A WORD?

Lord Jesus,
help me to think about you, learn
more about you, and love you today.

READ: MATTHEW 6:25–34

Do you know what an abbreviation is? An abbreviation is when you use a letter or a few letters instead of using the whole word.

AV stands for the Authorised Version of the Bible. This Bible was first printed in 1611 when James the Sixth of Scotland, and First of England, was king. It was authorised by him to be read in churches. That is how it came to be known as the 'authorised version'. Christians in other countries call it the 'King James Bible'.

Do you know what CV means? It means Curriculum Vitae. The words mean the course of your life – all the things that have happened to you. When you are older and apply for a job, you may be asked for a CV in which you tell what has happened in your life.

DV stands for two other Latin words: Deo Volente. These mean 'God willing'. Someone might say, 'We are going do this, DV.' 'We're going to do this, God willing – if God wants it to happen.'

One Friday morning I was in the United States and decided to e-mail a friend of mine. I said, 'I will get to Glasgow on Saturday at 8.45 a.m.' I also told him I was flying first into Chicago and then I was flying to Glasgow.

When I was flying into Chicago the wheels of the plane came down. We were about to touch down on the runway. But suddenly the plane went away up in the air again! We circled our way round Chicago. Finally the captain came on the intercom and said, 'You'll be wondering what happened.'

Well, we were wondering what happened! He said, 'As I was about to land, I saw there was another plane on the runway just in front of us.'

Help!

I suppose if he had waited another second or two, I might not have got back to Glasgow on Saturday morning. There would have been an accident instead. This reminded me that my life is not in my hands. It's in God's hands.

I thought to myself, 'I don't know what the future holds, but I know God holds my future. I must put my life in God's hands.'

It's safe to put our lives into God's hands. Although we don't know exactly what his will is for tomorrow, he knows. And he has promised never, ever, ever to leave us and never to forsake us.

So when you think of abbreviations like AV and CV remember that the best abbreviation of all is DV.

Lord Jesus

Although we don't know what will happen tomorrow, you know. You're with us today and you'll be with us tomorrow. You will be with us for all of our tomorrows. Help us to put our lives into your loving hands. All that you do for us is for our blessing. Please help us to trust you. We ask it in your name.

Amen.

15. GOD'S PATH

*Lord Jesus,
help me to think about you, learn
more about you, and love you today.*

READ: PSALM 77

When you go for a walk down a path how can you tell
that someone has been there before you? If I walked on
mud you would be able to see my footprints. But if you
could walk on the sea would you leave any footprints?
No you wouldn't.

Do you remember when God's people were taken out
of Egypt and across the sea? Read Psalm 77, verse 19.
This is one of the most interesting verses in the Book of
Psalms. It mentions how the Israelites were saved from
the Egyptians at the Red Sea and it tells us something
about God.

> Your way was through the sea, your
> path through the great waters; yet your
> footprints were unseen. You led your people

like a flock by the hand of Moses and Aaron
(Psalm 77:19-20 ESV).

Sometimes God works in our lives and leads us in ways that we don't understand. Sometimes we can't even see what he is doing.

Sometimes we can't understand what God is doing.

That's true especially when difficult things or sore things happen to us. However, when those difficult things happen we can still trust in God, even though we cannot understand what he is doing.

When you say, 'Where are you going, God? I can't see your footprints', he will say to you, 'Trust me, because I know what I am doing. I know where I am leading you. Follow me. One day you will see where my footprints were heading all the time.'

> I will remember the deeds of the LORD; yes, I will remember your wonders of old. I will ponder all your work, and meditate on your mighty deeds. Your way, O God, is holy. What god is great like our God? You are the God who works wonders; you have made known your might among the peoples (Psalm 77:11-14 ESV)

Loving Heavenly Father

We are thankful that you know everything about us, our past and our future. Even though we sometimes don't understand you, please help us to trust you. Thank you that you've shown us in Jesus that we can always trust you. Fill us with your joy and forgive our sins. We ask it for Jesus' sake.

Amen.

Lord Jesus,
help me to think about you, learn
more about you, and love you today.

READ: EPHESIANS 4:1-6

In Ephesians Chapter 4, verse 4, Paul says that the church is like a body. How is the church like a body?

What do we have on top of our bodies? A head. Now, if the church is a body, who do you think is the head? What happens in the head? The head is where all the orders come from. Who is head of the church? Jesus is the head of the church. So that's one way that the church is like a body. Bodies have got heads and Jesus is the head of the body. He's the one who tells us what to do.

There's another way the church is like a body. What happens if someone comes up to you with their fist clenched and punches you right in your face? What does your body do? It collapses. What do you do if somebody tries to do that to you? You protect yourself with your hands or with your arms.

If you get hurt in the leg or if you get kicked, does your hand go down to rub it? That is how a body works – when one part gets hurt, other parts of the body rush to help the part that's hurt.

That's also how the church works. When people in the church get hurt, the other parts of the body of Jesus rush to help and protect the part of the body that has been hurt or damaged.

What happens if you go to a football stadium and your team scores a goal? Does everybody just sit down and fold their arms? No. Their whole bodies stretch upwards and they shout – 'It's a goal!' People get excited and praise the team they support. That's how the body works. When something good happens, the whole body gets excited and says, 'Great!'

We belong to the body of Jesus, the church. When something great happens to someone who belongs to Jesus we say, 'That is absolutely wonderful!'

Because we all belong to the same body, we all have the same head who is Jesus. We care for each other when sad and bad things happen. We get excited for each other when wonderful and good things happen.

And that's what it means to belong to the body that is the church.

> There is one body and one Spirit, just as you were called in one hope of your calling (Ephesians 4:4).

Lord Jesus

Thank you that you have made us members of your body the church. Help us to care for one another, to love one another, to be happy or sad with each other. Thank you for all that you have done for us. We praise you today.

Amen.

17. A DAD AND HIS BOY

*Lord Jesus,
help me to think about you, learn
more about you, and love you today.*

READ: GENESIS 22:1-19

One day Abraham said to his son, Isaac, 'I am going to take you somewhere special and we are going to have a very special service.' The two of them went off. They got up early in the morning and rode away. They rode all day and they rode all the next day.

What do you think Isaac was saying? Probably, 'Are we there yet, Dad?'

Finally, they got to the foot of a mountain called Mount Moriah and they began to climb it. They had several things with them. Isaac was carrying some wood, because they were going to make a sacrifice to God. Abraham had the fire because they were going to burn the sacrifice. He also had a knife because in the Old Testament they killed the sacrifice.

No person or animal wants to be sacrificed. So Abraham also had ropes. He would use these to tie the sacrifice onto the altar that he was going to build.

When they were half way up the mountain, Isaac looked up at Abraham and said, 'Dad, I have got the wood, you've got the knife and the fire, but there is something missing. Where is the sacrifice?'

Abraham had a great secret he hadn't shared with his son. Isaac, himself, was going to be the sacrifice. But he couldn't tell Isaac about that yet, could he?

Instead, Abraham said, 'God will provide a sacrifice for us, Isaac. Let's keep going.'

Isaac kept going because he trusted his father, Abraham. He trusted him so much that, when they got to the top of the hill, he let his dad tie the ropes all round him.

Abraham stretched his son out on the altar. As Isaac looked up he saw that his dad had a knife in his hand. God had said, 'Go and sacrifice Isaac.'

Just as he was about to do it, God said, 'Stop!' When Abraham turned round, there in the bushes was an animal that God had provided. He took Isaac off the altar and put the animal on there instead.

Why should there be such a strange story in our Old Testament? Here is the reason. It is to tell us that Abraham didn't need to sacrifice Isaac, because God was going to sacrifice his Son, Jesus, to save us from our sins.

That mountain was called Moriah. It was the same place where later on, the city of Jerusalem was built. That was where Jesus made a sacrifice for our sins. Long before it happened, Abraham and Isaac were given a glimpse of what Jesus and his Father would do for us at Calvary.

Lord Jesus

We thank you that you were so brave and so obedient to your Father. You were willing to die on the cross to become our Saviour. Our Heavenly Father, we thank you that you sacrificed your Son for our sins. We love you more than ever and we want to be Jesus' followers. We pray in his name.

Amen.

Lord Jesus,
help me to think about you, learn
more about you, and love you today.

READ: JAMES 4:6; ROMANS 8:31

Each year I go to a very special dinner with some of my friends. We were all in the same class at school. One of these friends, whose name is David, used to live across the road from me when we were growing up.

After school we loved to play football together in the street. Those were the good old days when you could play football in the street without getting run down!

I had only one problem with David and that was his dad! He had been a really good football player. He often got home from work earlier than all the other dads. If we were playing football on the street, he'd join in. If David's dad was playing against your team, you had no chance of winning!

In the Bible, the book of James says, 'If God opposes you, you've no chance of winning.' Let's think about one of the teams that God is playing against. It's called 'Team Proud'.

God doesn't like it when we are proud. He is always on the other side. If you are proud then that's the team that you are on. You are on Team Proud – the losing team!

But there is good news.

> In Romans 8:31 Paul tells us, 'If God is for us, who can be against us?'

> In James 4:6 (ESV) it says, 'God opposes the proud but gives grace to the humble.'

So when we say to God, 'Oh God, there's still pride in my heart. Please help me to think about the Lord Jesus and how he was humble and not proud', then God says, 'I will be with you.'

No matter what happens to us, no matter what the opposition is, if God is for us we are on the winning side! The opposition to God will be defeated. Isn't that great!

Maybe at school someone will say, 'Where were you on Sunday?' Will you tell them that you were at Sunday

School? Perhaps they will laugh when you tell them. Remember this, God is for you. You will not be a loser if God is for you!

Loving Heavenly Father

Thank you that you're a God who loves the humble. We want to be humble. Sometimes we are proud and we don't depend on you. But deep down in our hearts we know that we are sinful. Please forgive us and be with us. We pray this in Jesus' name.

Amen.

19. GOD SAYS IT IS TIME

Lord Jesus,
help me to think about you, learn
more about you, and love you today.

READ: JOHN 7:25-31

One day some nasty people tried to seize Jesus. Can you imagine that? They hated the Lord Jesus so much that they wanted to get rid of him.

They were angry with Jesus, because of what he said and did. They tried to seize him, but 'his time' had not come. They couldn't get hold of him. Eventually, they would kill him. But on this occasion they couldn't do it. Jesus' 'time' had not yet come.

Do you know what that means?

It doesn't mean that Jesus looked through his bag and got out his clock and said, 'It's not time yet!' Jesus knew that there was a different kind of clock from the clocks that we use and the watches that we have.

God has his own time. And God had his own time for all the things that he wanted Jesus to do and all the things that would happen to Jesus. God had a plan in his mind for the whole of Jesus' life.

He had planned when Jesus would come into the world. Then at a certain time Jesus would die for our sins. Until God's time arrived, nobody could seize Jesus. God had his hand on everything that happened.

As these people were trying to seize Jesus it was as if God said, 'I'm not going to let you do that.' God's plan for Jesus was perfect.

God has a plan for his people – a marvellous one. God's plan always works out the way God wants. So when you get upset or when disappointing things happen, you can say, 'My Heavenly Father has a plan, and he's working out his plan for my life day by day. Somehow or other this must be part of God's plan for my life.'

So, as Christians we are able to look up into heaven and say, 'Heavenly Father, I don't really understand what's going on. But I know that you have a plan for my life. I know this must be a part of your plan. Help me to live for you so that one day I'll look back and say, "God did that. It was hard at the time, but God really knew what he was doing!"'

Lord Jesus

Thank you that you lived according to your dear Father's plan. We want to live according to his plan too. Please help us and guide us so that we may trust your Father and serve him. We ask it for your name's sake.

Amen.

20. TOO BUSY TO BE BORED

Lord Jesus,
help me to think about you, learn
more about you, and love you today.

READ: JOHN 16:5 – 16; ACTS 2:22-24

Do you ever get bored? Does your mum ever get bored? Perhaps your mum would say, 'I am far too busy ever to get bored.' Maybe that's part of the answer to the question, 'Does God ever get bored?' God might say, 'I'm far too busy looking after you to get bored!'

God's been looking after the world for a long time. He is still doing it today. So I don't think God ever gets bored. Is God ever lonely? He has to look after the whole universe, including you, all on his own. But God never gets lonely or bored because God is never on his own.

After three years teaching his disciples, Jesus let them into God's biggest secret. He is different from us. He is one God but three different persons: the Father, the Son and the Holy Spirit.

Even before he made the world, the Father was with his Son and with his Holy Spirit.

Is that hard for you to understand? It's hard for me to understand too! But we can be sure that God never gets bored because he always has company in himself. God the Father, the Son and the Holy Spirit.

Sometimes when you are with your friends, you forget what time it is. Suddenly, one of you will shout out, 'Look at the time! I was supposed to be home before now!' I think it must be like that for God the Father, with his Son and with his Holy Spirit. They enjoy each other so much that they never get bored.

However, there is something even more wonderful than that! The Father, Son and the Holy Spirit, one God, were talking together before the world was made. They knew we would sin and do wrong things. When they were talking about this, the Father said to the Son, 'Would you go into the world and die on a cross to save these people?' The Son said to the Father, 'Father, I'm willing to do that, but the Holy Spirit must also be sent into the world so that people will come to trust me and love me. He will give them power in their lives to live for me.' Peter spoke about this on the Day of Pentecost:

> Jesus of Nazareth ... being delivered by the determined purpose and foreknowledge of

God, you have taken by lawless hands, have crucified, and put to death; whom God raised up, having loosed the pains of death, because it was not possible that He should be held by it (Acts 2:22-24).

Through Jesus we get to know God as Father, Son and Holy Spirit. And when you know God you'll know that God never gets lonely or bored. But as well as that, you'll know that you will never be lonely. And you don't ever need to be bored when he is with you!

Lord Jesus

Please help us when we feel lonely to know that we are not on our own. Help us when we feel bored to realise that you have done so many wonderful things for us. We thank and praise you that you have become our Saviour.

Amen.

21. HIDE AND SEEK

*Lord Jesus,
help me to think about you, learn
more about you, and love you today.*

READ: GENESIS 3:1-19; PSALM 32: 7

I am sure you have played hide and seek for fun. But do you also hide in real life? Perhaps you don't want to go to school. You pull the duvet over your head and hide! You remember you haven't done your homework and you just want to run away. But you can't, can you?

We want to hide when we are afraid, or when we've done something wrong. We are afraid of what might happen to us if we are discovered. Most of us hide when we've done something wrong and we're afraid of being found out. We hope that if we hide, our problems will all go away.

Right at the beginning of the Bible, in Genesis Chapter 3, we read about what happened to Adam the first time he did something wrong. Adam and Eve both knew they had disobeyed God. They were frightened and so they hid from God.

Later on that day, God came to the Garden of Eden to speak with Adam, but Adam could not be found. God called out, 'Adam! Where are you?'

Foolish Adam was trying to hide from the God who had made the whole universe! Where was he hiding? Behind a bush! But the God who had made the whole universe had also made the bush that Adam was hiding behind. Was there any point in Adam trying to hide? No. The God he was trying to hide from could see everything.

God saw Adam and said, 'Adam, what are you doing behind that bush?' Adam said, 'I did something wrong and I was afraid.' That was why Adam hid.

But what should we do instead of hiding from God?

Instead we should hide beside God, as Psalm 32:7 tells us to do.

> You are my hiding place; You shall preserve me from trouble; You shall surround me with songs of deliverance.

David had been hiding from God for months because he'd done something very wrong. Finally he realised that he couldn't possibly hide from God. But there was somewhere he could hide. Instead of hiding from God, he could hide in God.

Have you ever done something that was wrong and hidden from your dad? Because you knew you couldn't hide from him forever, you thought of running away from home. But instead of running away, you ran to your dad and said, 'I'm sorry.'

Did he put his arms around you? Instead of having to hide from your dad anymore, you were hiding in him.

David realised that when you've done something wrong, God knows about it. We want to run away and hide because we're afraid that we've let God down. But instead of hiding from him, we should go and hide in him. He will put his arms around us and say, 'I forgive you and I'm going to help you.'

Heavenly Father

We thank you today that though we often want to hide from you because we sin, you love us and forgive us. We can hide in you. You are protecting us and you will bless us. We thank you in Jesus' name.

Amen.

Lord Jesus,
help me to think about you, learn
more about you, and love you today.

READ: PSALM 121

How much sleep do you need? Have you noticed how little babies seem to spend most of the time sleeping? If you have a little brother or sister, maybe sometimes you hear them crying in the middle of the night. Perhaps you wake up too or maybe you just turn over in bed and think, 'Well, mum and dad can look after the baby.'

When babies grow up they still wake people up, but this time they often wake up too early. Their mum and dad yawn and say, 'Get back to bed.' However, a few years after that, something very strange happens. Older children don't want to go to bed – isn't that right? But then in the morning they don't want to get up!

Albert Einstein was a very clever man. He spent a lot of time during the day thinking and working out problems.

He was a very clever scientist. After he died they decided to weigh his brain to find out how heavy it was. It was quite a bit heavier than the average brain! But because he spent a lot of time thinking with his brain, he also spent a lot of time sleeping. Albert Einstein needed ten hours sleep every night! Once he had spent all that time sleeping, he was refreshed and ready to spend lots of time thinking the next day.

Now, think about all the things God does. He is looking after our world. He is looking after the stars that we can see in the sky at night and the planets. Then there are all kinds of things we can't see. He is looking after those too. But, God doesn't need any sleep. He never gets tired, he never gets stuck, he never goes in the huff and says, 'I am going to bed and I'm not going to talk to anyone.'

Sometimes, mums get exhausted looking after just one baby. But God never ever, ever, ever gets exhausted, never gets tired, never gets sleepy. And he just loves to look after his children.

When you put your head down on the pillow to go to sleep, remember God is awake and he is watching over you. He will never ever take his eye off you. Isn't it wonderful to have a God who does not need sleep?

Lord God

We thank you that you are always awake and watching over us. You sent our Lord Jesus Christ to die for us. You will never stop watching over us or loving us. We love you, we trust you, we want to live for you. We pray for your blessing in Jesus our Saviour's name.

Amen.

23. WHEN DOES GOD ENJOY CHURCH?

Lord Jesus,
help me to think about you, learn
more about you, and love you today.

READ: MALACHI 1:10; 3:16–18; ZEPHANIAH 3:17

One day, Jesus went to the church in Capernaum. He was asked to preach that day. While he was preaching, there was a man full of an evil spirit who started shouting at him. I wonder if God enjoyed being in that service?

Sometimes, God doesn't enjoy being in church. How do I know that? Well, you can read about this in the very last book of the Old Testament. This is what God said to the people who were going to church in those days, 'I wish that somebody would come and shut the church doors. Although the people are coming to the building, they're not really coming to be with me which is the really important thing' (See Malachi 1:10).

Now, of course, we come to church to be with each other. But most of all we come to be with God. These people were just coming to church on the outside and not coming to God on the inside. So, there are some times when God doesn't really like coming to church. He'd rather somebody just shut the doors.

What happened next? Well, Malachi tells us that those who really loved the Lord talked about him with each other. The Lord listened and said, 'We need to write down the names of those who really trust me and love me. They will be mine in the day when I make up my treasure' (See Malachi 3:16-17).

So sometimes in Malachi's day, God didn't like going to church. But whenever the people were loving him and praising him and wanting to be with him, God loved being there. The prophet Zephaniah says:

> The LORD your God in your midst, The Mighty One, will save; He will rejoice over you with gladness, He will quiet you with His love, He will rejoice over you with singing (Zephaniah 3:17).

Did you know that God likes singing? Do you ever sing to God? Do you ever sing about how wonderful he is?

You listen to music and hum along because you like what you hear. Sometimes God is so happy, because we're praising him, that he sings along with us because he loves to hear us singing.

Can you really believe that God loves you as much as that? Well, since he sent his Son to die for us, we can be absolutely sure that he loves us that much.

So, when you're singing to God in church or in Sunday School, ask this question, 'Does the Lord like my singing today? Am I really praising him or am I grumpy?'

Think about whether your singing is pleasing God, because if it is, God is singing along with you.

Lord Jesus

We thank you that you love us and we pray that you will love to hear us sing about your goodness, power and faithfulness. Help us not only to enjoy being together but to enjoy being with you and praising you. We ask this in your name.

Amen.

24. WHAT IS A REVIVAL?

Lord Jesus,
help me to think about you, learn
more about you, and love you today.

READ: ACTS 8:1-8

A long time ago, two boys lived in a town called Coleraine in Northern Ireland. Let's call them Jimmy and Sammy. God was working in this city. One day when the two boys were in their classroom at school, Jimmy was very upset. All of a sudden he just burst into tears.

Let's call their teacher Mrs McClutchie. She sighed and said to him, 'Come out here, Jimmy.' Jimmy shuffled up to her big high desk where she quietly asked him, 'Jimmy, what's wrong with you, today?' This is what Jimmy said, 'Mrs McClutchie, I am so sad because of my sins.'

Well, Mrs McClutchie didn't know what to say. Jimmy was still crying. After a few moments, Mrs McClutchie decided that Jimmy should go back home to speak to his mum and dad.

She pointed to Sammy who was still sitting at his desk. 'Sammy,' she said, 'close your books, put them on the desk and you take Jimmy home.'

Now Sammy had been worried about his sins as well. But he had told the Lord Jesus about them. He had said to Jesus, 'Lord Jesus, please forgive my sins and make me clean in my heart and help me to serve you.' So Sammy was already a Christian. He knew just what to say to help Jimmy.

'Jimmy, if you trust the Lord Jesus and ask him to forgive you, he'll forgive all your sins. We should pray to Jesus about your sins right now.' And that's exactly what they did. They prayed together, 'Lord Jesus, thank you for dying for Jimmy on the cross. He wants to have his sins forgiven and he wants to trust you.'

Jimmy began to trust the Lord Jesus. The next day at school, Mrs McClutchie was absolutely amazed. She said, 'What's happened? 'Oh Mrs McClutchie,' Jimmy exclaimed. 'I'm so happy because my sins have all been forgiven!'

Mrs McClutchie wasn't sure what to say to Jimmy so she told him to get on with his work. But just then another boy put his hand up and said, 'Please Miss, may I leave the room?' Then another boy did the same. Then one of the girls, 'Please Miss, may I leave the room?'

Within half an hour almost everybody had left. None of them came back. Mrs McClutchie didn't know what to think. So she stood up on her chair and looked out of the window. All the boys and girls in the class were sitting on the ground praying that the Lord Jesus would forgive their sins.

Mrs McClutchie immediately went to get the minister. It didn't take long for the news to spread. Mums and dads and many other people began to turn up at the school. They saw what was happening and soon they were asking the boys and girls, 'How can we get our sins forgiven?' Nobody left the school until 11 o'clock at night. Many of them went home happy that their sins had been forgiven.

Now if somebody in your school were to say to you, 'I'm so unhappy about all the wrong things I've done,' would you be able to tell them about the Lord Jesus? I hope so.

Lord Jesus

We thank you that sometimes you do these amazing things. If you do an amazing thing like that in somebody we know, help us to be able to tell them that they need you as their Saviour. We ask this in your name.

Amen.

25. THE SUFFERINGS OF JESUS

Lord Jesus,
help me to think about you, learn
more about you, and love you today.

READ: JOHN 19:1−3

When you think about all the horrible things people did to the Lord Jesus, do you ever ask, 'Why did God let that happen?' There is a reason for Jesus' sufferings.

When people died by being crucified, it took a long time. One of the things that the Romans did in order to shorten that time was to beat the people they were going to crucify. That meant that they would die more quickly.

We know what they did to their prisoners because we read about this in the Gospels. This is what they did to Jesus Christ.

We also read about it in other places. The Romans, themselves, wrote down what they did to their prisoners.

In the Gospels and in these other books, we can find out exactly what they did to the Lord Jesus Christ before his crucifixion.

Pontius Pilate gave the orders to have Jesus flogged. His soldiers stripped him. They then took a whip which had sharp little stones and pieces of metal in it. A very strong man, or perhaps several men, started to beat Jesus across the back – again and again and again. That must have been terrible – absolutely terrible.

> So then Pilate took Jesus and scourged Him. And the soldiers twisted a crown of thorns and put it on His head, and they put on Him a purple robe. Then they said, 'Hail, King of the Jews!' And they struck Him with their hands (John 19:1-3).

Why did God let that happen? Couldn't God have sent some angels to save Jesus? Well, he could have. Jesus himself said, 'God could send thousands of angels to save me if I asked him to stop this.' So why did God let that happen? Why did Jesus let that happen to him?

The answer to that question is this: Jesus went through all that because he loves you. Isn't it absolutely amazing that the Lord Jesus was prepared to suffer so much, to die in our place, to take away our sins just because he loves us so much?

Lord Jesus

We can hardly bear to think about the terrible things you suffered. We want to thank and praise you that you loved us so much, that you were prepared to be our Saviour. May we always love, serve and obey you. We ask this for your sake.

Amen.

26. MASTER CRAFTSMAN

Lord Jesus,
help me to think about you, learn
more about you, and love you today.

READ: JOHN 5:19–24; JOHN 1:3

When Jesus came into the world, who were the two people who looked after him? One was, of course, his mother, Mary, and the other was Joseph. What did Joseph do for a living? How did he make money to feed his family? He was a carpenter.

I am sure that when Jesus was a little boy he went into Joseph's carpenter's shop to watch him work. John 5: 19 is one of my favourite verses in the Bible. It reminds us that Jesus' love for his stepfather, Joseph, was just a small version of his love for his Heavenly Father.

In those days, if a father was a carpenter then his son probably became a carpenter. So, this is why Jesus says, 'The Son does what he sees his Father doing.'

> Then Jesus answered and said to them, 'Most assuredly, I say to you, the Son can do nothing of Himself, but what He sees the Father do; for whatever He does, the Son also does in like manner' (John 5:19).

Joseph made things with his hands and he was a master craftsman. If someone had gone into Joseph's carpenter's shop and said, 'Excuse me, I want to meet the master craftsman,' I suppose Joseph would have said, 'That's me. I'm the master craftsman here. My name is above the door. I can make anything you want. I can build you a house of wood. I could make you a rocking horse. I could make you a chair or a table. I could make you anything out of wood because I am the master craftsman.'

If you had gone into that carpenter's shop and seen Jesus, you would have thought, 'This boy must be the master craftsman's apprentice who is just learning the trade.' But the truth of the matter was that it was Joseph who was the apprentice and Jesus who was the master craftsman! The Bible tells us that everything in the world was made by Jesus!

> All things were made through Him, and without Him nothing was made that was made (John 1:3.

That is really hard to understand, isn't it? The one who made everything was sitting beside Joseph's bench watching him make things with wood. Joseph was a master craftsman with wood, but he was really just learning how to be Jesus' apprentice. All through his life, the Lord Jesus would show Joseph how to be an apprentice to the person who had created the whole world.

So, will you remember that Jesus is the person who made the whole world? The little baby who was lying in the manger was the person who made the wood for the manger and made the whole world.

If he can do that, he can do anything, can't he?

Lord Jesus

We thank you that, although you are very great and powerful, you became very small and weak for us. We pray that when we are made to feel small, we will remember that the Saviour we have is great and is the Creator of all things. We ask it for your name's sake.

Amen.

27. GOD'S LANGUAGE

*Lord Jesus,
help me to think about you, learn
more about you, and love you today.*

READ: JOHN 1:1–14

How many languages can you speak? People in the
United Kingdom, America, Australia, New Zealand,
Canada and other places speak English. Can you speak
other languages too? Some people speak German,
Dutch, French, Italian and Spanish. In Scotland,
there is another language that some people speak. It
is called Gaelic.

Now here is another question. Do you think God
understands all these languages? Yes, he does! He
understands all languages, so that whenever anybody
prays in one of these different languages, God hears
that language and answers prayer.

When we speak, we use words. But do you know a
language where you do not speak any words? Sign

language doesn't use spoken words. This is a language that is used by people who cannot hear. When someone is speaking with sign language they use their hands instead of their tongue. All the words have special hand signs.

There is another kind of language we sometimes use – it is the kind of language you use when your parents ask you to do something and you put an angry scowl on your face. It's the kind of language you use if you are trying to do something and it doesn't work. Your face scrunches up and you stamp your feet! It's the kind of language you use when you say goodbye to your mum and dad when you really wish you were going with them. Your face is all crumpled up and your mouth is down at the ends.

What kind of language do we call that? It's called 'body language'. It's a kind of sign language that shows what we really think.

If we are happy, what kind of body language do we use? We smile. If we are sad, what kind of body language do we use? We look sad – or we frown.

Did you know that God has used body language? The Lord Jesus is God's body language. Even if we cannot understand other languages, the most important language to understand is God's body language.

God sent his Son to take a human body and to live in a human body. In this way, we see what the invisible God is like.

> And the Word became flesh and dwelt among us, and we beheld His glory, the glory as of the only begotten of the Father, full of grace and truth (John 1:14).

Because Jesus was sent by God, we can understand what God is really like. God's Son took a human body and died on the cross. So God's body language tells us that he loves us more than anything.

> He came to His own, and His own did not receive Him. But as many as received Him, to them He gave the right to become children of God, to those who believe in His name (John 1:11-12).

Lord Jesus

We thank you that you have shown us what you are really like. You died for us on the cross in order to forgive our sins and to make us new. You rose again from the dead to be our living Saviour for evermore. Help us to trust you. We ask this for your great name's sake.

Amen.

28. ANOTHER JOURNEY THROUGH TIME

Lord Jesus,
help me to think about you, learn
more about you, and love you today.

READ: JOHN 17:24; EPHESIANS 1:4; 1 PETER 1:20

Imagine that you are in the time machine again. After a few minutes you see Queen Victoria! Suddenly, you look out of the window and see Columbus sailing across the Atlantic. Then it's the year 1314 and outside the Battle of Bannockburn is being fought.

All of a sudden you see a shining light in the distance! It's Bethlehem and you've reached Bible times! Then you zoom past Daniel and the lions and David with his sheep. You see Moses, Joseph and Abraham for just a few minutes. The time machine begins to slow down. You have gone right back to the beginning of the Bible.

Just as Adam and Eve begin to disappear you see a brilliant flash of light and the whole world disappears. There is nothing to be seen ... and then you hear a voice.

God the Father is speaking to his Son. Let's listen to what is said: 'After we've made them,' he says, 'they're going to sin.' 'Father, we'll have to rescue them,' is the Son's reply. The Father says to his Son, 'Yes, let's make a plan.' 'Father,' says the Son, 'We can share the plan.' I think we can hear the Holy Spirit saying, 'I'll help too.' God the Father then announces, 'Here is the plan …'

On the time machine screen you see a picture of a manger. What does that mean?

God the Father says, 'Son, you will need to become a baby and go to the smallest and the poorest. Only when you do this and live a perfect life from the beginning, will we be able to rescue people from their sins. Will you do that? Will you become a baby in a manger?' 'Father,' says the Son, 'Of course, I will.'

Another picture appears on the screen. It's a star. Why would God need a star?

God the Father said, 'I will send a star because I want wise men from the east to follow it. They won't have a Bible. They won't know very much about you. But they can follow a new star. I want people from all over the world to learn about how you will rescue them. Will you go into the world and be the Saviour?' The Son says, 'Father, of course! I'll go into the world.'

'My Son,' God the Father says, 'there is a third part of the plan. It is a cross.'

Now why would God the Father need a cross?

'This plan needs a cross,' says the Father, 'because only if you are prepared to die for the sins of the world will it be possible for us to rescue them from their sins. I will bring you back to life, but you must first die on the cross for their sins to save them. Would you do that for them? Would you do that for me?' The Son says to his Father, 'Of course. I will do it. And the plan will work.'

Of course you don't need a time machine to find out about the plans God made. We read about them in God's Word, the Bible. We read about Jesus and about how the plan God made worked out. But if we really did have a time machine, we'd turn back for home now and we'd be talking together for ages about everything we had seen and heard.

Lord Jesus

Thank you that you were willing to follow God the Father's plan. You were willing to come as a baby, to live in the world and to die for sinners on the cross. Thank you for this perfect plan of salvation. We pray this in your name.

Amen.

29. INSIDE OUTSIDE

*Lord Jesus,
help me to think about you, learn
more about you, and love you today.*

READ: 1 SAMUEL 16:7

When King David was a very young boy, somebody important came to his house – the most important minister in the country. His name was Samuel and Samuel said to David's father, Jesse, that God was going to make the next king and so he wanted to see all of his sons. So David's father called them in, one by one.

When Samuel saw the first one, he thought, 'This must be the one.' But God said, 'It's not this one.' They went through all the boys and God kept saying to him, 'It's not this one.' And so Samuel said to Jesse, 'Do you have any other boys?'

There was one, a young lad, not as tall or as important as the others, but he was the only one who wasn't there.

'Oh,' Jesse said, 'there's David. He's out in the fields, looking after the sheep. You don't want to see David.'

But the Lord said to Samuel, when David came in, 'This is the boy who is going to be king.'

There were some words that God taught Samuel that day, words that we should learn too. These teach us that people look at the outside, but God looks at the inside.

> For the LORD does not see as man sees; for man looks at the outward appearance, but the LORD looks at the heart (1 Samuel 16:7).

We all tend to look on the outside don't we? You wonder, if you're a girl, 'Am I going to be pretty?' Or if you're a boy, 'Am I going to be handsome.' But the Lord Jesus never, ever, ever, ever looks just at what you're like on the outside. What's most important is not if you're big or if you're small, if you're beautiful or not very beautiful. He looks right into the heart and that's the only thing that He really cares about, because all those who love Jesus are one day going to be fabulously beautiful and wonderfully handsome and strong.

Just now, the most important thing God wants to find in you is a love and a trust for him. Sometimes, it's a bit hard if you don't look very great, I know that. But if you can say, 'Lord Jesus, I trust you. You love me so much

I want to be your disciple.' That's the first thing that really matters to the Lord Jesus. Isn't that great? Let's pray and thank Jesus for looking right into our hearts to see our love for him.

Lord Jesus

We do love you, we do trust you. We know from your Word that this is what you love most of all. And so we pray that you would help us to love and serve you more. We ask all this in your name.

Amen.

30. A NEW WORD

Lord Jesus,
help me to think about you, learn
more about you, and love you today.

READ: ACTS 11:19-26

When I started school, a very long time ago, we often used to learn new words. I think we had to learn one every day. I had a friend who tried to learn even more than that. He would try to learn five new words. He always had a new word for any situation – it was quite annoying!

Now, here's a question. If there is a word you hear and you don't know what it means, what kind of book do you go to? A dictionary would be a good idea. I've got quite a lot of dictionaries and some of them are very big. One of them is called the Oxford English Dictionary. All the words in the English language are in that dictionary. There are two volumes.

You would think that you would need more books than two volumes to keep all the words in the English language? But the dictionary publishers did something unusual. On every page they printed four pages! And the print is so small the dictionary comes with a magnifying glass to help you read it!

So, whenever I hear a word that I've never heard before, I can go to the dictionary and find out exactly what it means.

Now, you probably have lots of friends who don't really know what the word 'Christian' means, so how are they going to find out? They might not have a dictionary. And perhaps your friends don't ever read the Bible. But there is another way for them to discover the meaning of this word.

If they looked at you and really found out everything about you, they might be able to say, 'My, he's a follower of Jesus, she's a follower of Jesus.'

By watching your life, they would be able to learn what it really means to be a Christian. Instead of having to go to the Oxford English Dictionary, they could come to you and say, 'How do I become a Christian like you?' That's exactly what happened in Antioch. Let's pray that will happen where we live too.

> And the hand of the Lord was with them,
> and a great number believed and turned to
> the Lord (Acts 11:21).

Loving Heavenly Father

We thank you that you speak to us through your Word in the Bible. We thank you, too, that by your Spirit, you are able to make us more and more like Jesus. Please may our friends and family see your love in our lives and want to become Christians too. We pray in Jesus' name.

Amen.

31. WHAT ARE ANGELS FOR?

*Lord Jesus,
help me to think about you, learn
more about you, and love you today.*

READ: GENESIS 3:24; LUKE 2:13

What are angels for? They bring messages from heaven to earth. That's why they are called angels. Angel doesn't mean that you are especially good, but it means that you are a messenger. That's what the word really means.

We know there are different kinds of angels. There is at least one special one called an archangel – a chief angel. And there are other angels: seraphim (in Hebrew seraphim is plural and seraph is singular).

The very first angels to appear in the Bible are called cherubim. What did the cherubim do when they first appeared? What were they holding in their hands? They were holding flaming swords. Why were they holding flaming swords? Because they were guarding the way to the Garden of Eden. Why did they need to guard the way? Because Adam and Eve had been driven out of the Garden, from the Lord's presence, because of their sin.

> So He drove out the man; and He placed cherubim at the east of the garden of Eden, and a flaming sword which turned every way, to guard the way to the tree of life (Genesis 3:24).

Then, at Christmas time, when the angels came, their message was: God is opening the way back. They must have been very excited.

> And suddenly there was with the angel a multitude of the heavenly host praising God and saying: 'Glory to God in the highest, And on earth peace, goodwill toward men!' (Luke 2:13-14).

Imagine waiting all that time – thousand of years – before the Garden of Eden could be opened again. No wonder the angels were excited at Christmas time. Did you know that Jesus said, 'I am the door'? He is the One who opens the door back into the presence of God.

> I am the door. If anyone enters by Me, he will be saved, and will go in and out and find pasture (John 10:9).

Do you know this song?

> There's a way back to God
> From the dark paths of sin.
> There's a door that is open
> And you may go in
> At Calvary's cross is where you begin
> When you come as a sinner to Jesus.
>
> (E H Swinstead)

No wonder the angels burst out of heaven after waiting so long for Jesus to open the door for us to go in. Have you gone in or are you still outside?

Lord Jesus

Thank you that you came to open the way to heaven for everyone who trusts in you. We thank you for the excitement the angels must have felt when you came from heaven to earth. We pray that through faith in you, loving you and serving you, we may know that we belong to you and that you will look after us. We pray this in your name.

Amen.

Conclusion

Well, you have made it right to the end of the book! Well done! I hope you have enjoyed it and that it has helped you to think about the Lord Jesus, to trust him, and to love him more.

Most of the books I have written are for grown-ups. So why does someone who writes for grown-ups want to write books for children as well? There are lots of reasons, but since we're at the end of the book now, maybe I should mention only two.

The first is that when the Lord Jesus was on earth he loved children and children loved him. And that's still true! He wants you to know that, and he wants you to trust him as your Saviour and love him as your Lord. Books about him can help us to do that. I hope this one has helped you.

The second reason is this. Although I am a grown-up, I was once one of the children who needed to learn about Jesus' love for me. And so, when I was your age, I started reading the Bible each day, and asking the Lord to help me to understand it. I hope you will do the same. The Bible is a big book—actually there are sixty-six books in it—and I needed help to read it and understand it. Two books you might find helpful are *66 Books One Story* and *Read With Me*.[1]

---

1. Paul Reynolds, *66 Books One Story*, (Christian Focus Publications, Tain, Ross-shire, Scotland, 2013) ISBN: 978-1-84550-819-7.
Jean Stapleton, *Read With Me*, (Christian Focus Publications, Tain, Ross-shire, Scotland, 2006) ISBN: 978-1-84550-148-8.

So I hope you will start reading the Bible when you are young. But try not to make the mistake I did! I thought that reading the Bible each day was the same thing as being a Christian. It was a while before I realised that although that's important, it's not the same as knowing and trusting the Lord Jesus himself. Then, one day, I was reading the words of Jesus in John's Gospel Chapter 5 verses 39-40. He said to some people who were listening to him: 'You search the Scriptures, for in them you think you have eternal life; and these are they which testify of Me. But you are not willing to come to Me that you may have life.' I realised that Jesus was not just speaking to people long ago who made that mistake. I had made it too. He was speaking to me!

I knew then that I must pray that he would help me to come to him, to trust him, and to get to know him. Some time later, Jesus' words in John's Gospel chapter 8, verse 12 helped me to do that: 'Then Jesus spoke to them again, saying, "I am the light of the world. He who follows Me shall not walk in darkness, but have the light of life."' He has kept his promise!

So now you know why I wanted to write this book! And now I hope you will want to read the very best book—the Bible— yourself. Maybe you could start by reading John's Gospel.

May you know the love and presence of the Lord Jesus every day!

Sinclair B. Ferguson

Like the Savior, Sinclair clearly loved the children he pastored and pastored the children he loved. The questions and illustrations and historical anecdotes will pique the interest of parent and child alike. Another great book to help our children spend time thinking about how Jesus loves them.

Jonny Gibson,
Associate Professor of Old Testament,
Westminster Theological Seminary;
Author of *The Moon Is Always Round*

From the time they are infants, children learn to sing 'Jesus loves me this I know, for the Bible tells me so.' Yet, many children do not understand how Jesus loves them. This devotional book for young men and women is a delightful companion to help them learn the way in which Jesus loves them and how they can know and rest in his love for them. It is filled with fun and enjoyable stories that engage young readers while helping to disciple them in their love of our Savior.

Burk Parsons
Senior Pastor of Saint Andrew's Chapel
and Editor of Tabletalk Magazine

Books in this series

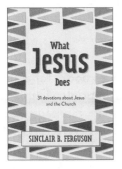

What Jesus Does
31 Devotions about Jesus and the Church
ISBN: 978-1-5271-0731-1

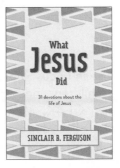

What Jesus Did
31 Devotions about the Life of Jesus
ISBN: 978-1-5271-0799-1

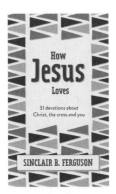

How Jesus Loves
31 Devotions about Christ, the cross and you
ISBN: 978-1-5271-0858-5

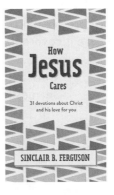

How Jesus Cares
31 Devotions about Christ and his love for you
ISBN: 978-1-5271-0859-2